The Straight Forward No Nonsense Single Mom Devotional

Dr. Sophia Reed

Copyright © 2018 by Sophia Reed
www.sophie-sticatedmom.com
ISBN: 978-1-9810919-4-2
All rights reserved. This book or any portion thereof
may not be reproduced or used in any manner whatsoever
without the express written permission of the author except for
the use of brief quotations in a book review.

About Me

Hello fellow single moms, and thank you so much for buying my book. My name is Dr. Reed, or you can just call me Sophia, and I am the author of this devotional. You may or may not know me from my blog (Sophie-sticated Mom) www.sophie-sticatedmom.com. No matter if you do or don't, I am still going to take the time to share some things about myself and the purpose of this book.

I started this whole journey of inspiring women, because I was once in a place where you may be today. There were times of struggle, feeling stuck, wondering when things were going to get better, and just feeling I was called to do bigger and better things but not knowing how I would get there.

I was this single mom, sitting around, day in and day out, being unhappy, unfulfilled, unsatisfied, and thinking that there had to be more to life than this. But everyone in my life told me that I should just sit down and be happy with what I had. No one could understand the high dreams that I had for myself and the dreams that God was feeding into my heart. They thought I was doing way too much and I wanted way too much.

But how many of you know that God gave the dream to you and not them? God told me to dream bigger. Why should I be limited as a single mom or as a woman? Why can't my life be just as awesome as the next? Who says that single mothers have to get the short end of the stick? Where is there a rule book that says, just because you are a single mom, you are bound to be single forever, struggling, lonely, overwhelmed, tired, and wishing upon a star that things will get better for you?

That is when I decided to stop living by what other people thought I should do and start living by my own rules, allowing God to guide my decisions. I went from feeling unfulfilled to having purpose, and I have not looked back since. So now I encourage all women, especially single mothers, to make boss moves while keeping God first. To not feel limited by the situation they are in or defined by their circumstances.

If I can find a better way with how jacked up, smart-mouthed, and sinful I used to be, I promise you can too. If I can do it, then you can do it. Now that we got that out of the way, know that when I wrote this devotional, I had all these things in mind. It is my hope that it can be a guide to encourage and motivate you as a single mom.

I am a real type of woman. God talks to me in a real type of way and that is exactly the type of message I want to relay in this 30-day devotional. Expect some no-nonsense advice, Godly advice, and for me to keep it real with you. Enjoy reading this book and don't forget to pay my blog a visit at www.sophie-sticatedmom.com.

I almost forgot, for those of you who care, I can spout out my credentials to show you guys I have some depth and to demonstrate what God did for me. I have a master's degree in marriage and family therapy, I am a National Certified Counselor, and I have a PhD in Human Behavior.

Happy reading.

~Day 1~
The Past Does Not Define You

My single-mother story is terrible. I will not go into too much detail, but it involved a wife and a girlfriend, plus my son's father being incarcerated for seven years. I think that is just enough information to let you know how insane that situation was, without making this whole chapter about re-visiting the past. Instead I want to focus on how you can move away from it.

The only reason I am even going into my past situation is because so often, when people look at me, they do not think that my past would consist of so much drama. I am now this women with three degrees, who looks put together and composed; who would have thought her past consisted of so much… rachetness, for a lack of a better word?

I tell you this, because I want you to know that the past does not define your present or your future. You may be a divorcee, a widow, a one-night stand, a woman that has never been married, or a woman who became a mother through an unplanned pregnancy. It does not matter.

What does matter is today. Today is a new day, yesterday is gone and passed away. And with every renewing day, you have an opportunity to re-invent yourself. But the key to stepping into your future is letting go of the past. I do not care if you used to be a drug addict, a prostitute, or a promiscuous person. As long as it is in the past, let it stay there and do not let it continue to come into your now.

The most famous trick about Satan is that he loves to remind you of who you use to be.

Remember when you had a child out of wedlock, remember when your marriage did not work out and you got a divorce, remember when you were a bad wife, remember that you are the reason why your child's father is not in your child's life, remember when you used to sleep around, remember, remember, remember?

> *"Submit yourselves, then, to God. Resist the devil, and he will flee from you." James 4:7*

Do not feed into the devil, do not allow the devil to lie to you or remind you of who you use to be or what you did. Call out these thoughts. The devil is trying to get into your head, mess up your day, and ultimately mess up your future. And he uses the past to do that.

Instead of paying too much attention to the devil, you need to pay enough attention to God. And the Word tells us that,

> *"For as high as the heavens are above the earth, so great is His love for those who fear Him; as far as the east is from the west, so far has He removed our transgressions from us." Psalm 103:11-12*

All this really means is, once you confess your sins, come to your senses, fear God, and are aware of your wrongdoings, God will remember your sins no more. *"As far as the east is from the west."* Which is extremely far. So, if God is willing to not remember what you have done,

Day 1: *The Past Does Not Define You*

do not allow the devil to come in and convict you and do not allow yourself to come in and convict yourself. Move forward from the past, because there is no changing it.

Daily Prayer

Lord,

I confess my sins. Whatever I have done that is not of You, I want to confess it to You and know that, with all my heart, You have forgiven me. And if there is anything from my past that I am not aware of that offends You, then I pray that You bring it to my mind so I can repent for those sins as well.

Whatever I have done, whoever I was, and whatever I have been through that is NOT of You, I pray for Your forgiveness, and I ask You to guide my steps so I do not continue to make bad decisions. I know I am forgiven and know that I am not condemned in Your eyes, so I will no longer condemn myself. And I also will not let Satan convict me of my past wrongdoings any further. For by Your grace, I am forgiven.

In Jesus' name I pray. Amen.

~Day 2~
Being a Single Mom is Nothing New

Often times, when people think of single moms, the last thing they think of is the Bible. Did single motherhood even exist back then? It did, which is why I want to share two women with you who were single mothers to show you that God has not forgotten about you. God does not condemn you for being a single mother, and He is ready to step in and help you anytime you need it. God is love, He created you, and He has no choice but to love you.

Elijah and the widow at Zarephath (Kings 17:7-16)

God sent Elijah to the widow at Zarephath, where God told him he would be provided for by a widow with a son. But when Elijah got to the widow, even though God has sent him, he was not greeted with open arms. Instead he was greeted with this:

> *"'As surely as the Lord your God lives,' she replied, 'I don't have any bread—only a handful of flour in a jar and a little olive oil in a jug. I am gathering a few sticks to take home and make a meal for myself and my son, that we may eat it—and die.'" 1 Kings 17:12*

In other words, she and her son were starving, and she was not in the mood to feed someone else. Have you ever been in a situation like this as a single mother?

Day 2: *Being a Single Mom is Nothing New*

Struggling, no money, barely putting food on the table, wondering how you are going to feed your kids, thinking that, if money does not come from somewhere soon, you and your children are just going to lay down and die!

Imagine the desperation this mother must have felt by not being able to provide for herself or her son. Everything according to the world's way of thinking would have told her not to feed Elijah, because she barely had food for herself. But the widow chose not to believe her eyes but to stand up on faith. Her eyes told her there would be no more food, but her faith told her God would make a way. And with that, she gave food to Elijah. Her gesture caused her to be blessed, and she did not run out of food again.

"So there was food every day for Elijah and for the woman and her family. For the jar of flour was not used up and the jug of oil did not run dry, in keeping with the word of the Lord spoken by Elijah." 1 Kings 17:15-16

What we can learn from the widow is that God has your back. You may be tired, broke, struggling, out of food, or about to get your utilities turned off. Just remember that God has not forgotten about you. Remember this widow and remember that she thought she and her son would just sit, starve, and die. And there was nothing she could do about that in the physical realm. What she chose to do instead was to put her last bit of faith in God and God came through for her.

Abraham and Hagar (Genesis 16)

In the story of Abraham and Hagar, most people feel sorry for Sarah, the woman who was barren, and see Hagar as some home-wrecking woman who had the child God did not promise. But let's not forget, Hagar was commanded to sleep with Abraham by Sarah. And once Sarah grew tired of Hagar and her son, due to pure jealousy, God commanded Abraham to send both Hagar and Ishmael out into the desert. Because Hagar's son, Ishmael, was not Abraham's chosen child.

Put yourself in Hagar's shoes for a minute here. She was forced to sleep with Abraham, forced to have a baby for Sarah, and then she was forced out into the desert. With no husband, no father for her child, a small amount of food, and a bottle of water.

"Early the next morning Abraham got some food and a bottle of water. The bottle was made out of animal skin. He gave the food and water to Hagar, placing them on her shoulders. Then he sent her away with the boy. She went on her way and wandered in the Desert of Beersheba." Genesis 21:14

How long was a bottle of water really going to last in the desert? It surely sounds like this was a death sentence to me. And so did Hagar, because as her son lay dying in the desert, there was nothing she could do to ease his pain. Then the Lord spoke:

"What is the matter, Hagar? Do not be afraid. God has heard the boy crying as he lies there. Lift up the boy and take him by the hand. I will make him into a great nation." Genesis 21:17-19

No, Ishmael was not the promised child. Yes, Hagar was "technically" an adulteress. But God, being the God that we serve, chose to have mercy on them both. And it was in the desert that He chose to hear Hagar's cries for her son.

Day 2: *Being a Single Mom is Nothing New*

The desert is such a symbolic place. It is a place that is normally hot and devoid of water. It is a place where Hagar and her son were sent to die. It is a place where they could have just sat, knowing that it was very likely no one would come by and save them. But it was the place where Hagar chose to pray, because that was the only option she had.

How many of you are in the desert? In a dry and barren place, not knowing when or if someone is going to even come by and save you? Instead of trying to fix it all on your own, cry out to God like Hagar did and let Him fix it.

I encourage you to read both of the above stories and derive your own meaning from them. As a single mother, sometimes it feels that we are in the desert, that we are about to die, that more is put on us than we can bear, that we do not know what we will do next, or that we have been forsaken. Even if you feel all alone or like everyone has turned their back on you, know that God has not turned His back on you and never will. Just cry out to Him.

Like the widow, your current situation may be bad and you may not know how to make ends meet. Do not give up, God could be sending an Elijah right now that can turn your situation around. All you have to do is believe.

Lord,

I know that you love me, and I know that I have a special place in Your heart. For the Word says, *"Whoever touches me is touching the apple of God's eye."* (Zechariah 2:8) Therefore, I know that what I am going through now, whatever hardships are awaiting me in the near future, and whatever people or situations have tried to shut me down, they will not shut me up. I will continue to praise You with my mouth, knowing You will come through. I trust You to handle my situation, be my redeemer, and fight my battles. I release whatever I am going through into Your hands.

In Jesus' name I pray. Amen.

~*Day 3*~

Talk to God

Have you ever just talked to God? And when I say talk to God, I mean have a conversation. Just let out all of your frustrations, grievances, hurts, pains, and anger—even if you are angry at God Himself?

What I have come to learn about God is the more you let it out to God, the more you are inviting God to come in and heal your pain. So do not be afraid to offend God by what you are saying and how you feel. He already knows, and the sooner you talk to Him about it, the sooner He can heal you.

As a single mother, maybe you thought you would be married by now. You thought your child would have a good father instead of a deadbeat one. You thought you would have stayed married. You thought your husband would have loved you forever. You thought that you would have loved your husband forever. You thought that God would have healed your marriage. You thought you would be one big happy family, and now that has all washed away.

You can be mad about the things that you thought would happen, but you do not need to stay mad about those things. There is no need to put on a strong face for God or to pretend to be like Mother Teresa praying for world peace. If there is something bothering you, let God know about it, because He already knows and He is just waiting for you to tell Him.

Have you ever had a friend, boyfriend, or even a husband, and you just knew something was bothering them? But instead of speaking to you about it, they talked to other people behind your back or just walked around with an attitude pretending like everything was all good?

Don't be like that with God. God is your father and He is the closest ally you have. More than any boyfriend, relative, or friend. So if you feel like you can talk to all those people, then you need to feel comfortable talking to God. Because He is the only one who can fix what you are going through.

Become a friend of God. Let go of all those superficial prayers and sayings that you think God wants to hear or what you think a Christian is supposed to say. Don't be fake with God. The only way a relationship can grow and get deeper is if there is trust and honesty. That is the type of relationship you want to form with God.

Daily Prayer

Today, there is no assigned prayer. Instead, I want you to open up your heart and allow God in. Get into your quiet place and air all of your issues, grievances, disappointments, all of it. Do not hold back. Get used to talking to God in this way, for this is the purest form of prayer that you can have with Him.

~Day 4~
Let It Go

A lot of times, as single mothers, it can be hard to let go of the past. You may be wondering why your child's father or your ex-husband does not want you anymore. Why he does not want to be involved with the child's life. Why you made the decision to marry him. Why you made the decision to have a child by him. Why God let your child's father pass away.

Why did your ex hit you? Or better yet, why did you allow him to hit you? Why did you allow him to verbally abuse you? Or tear you down? Or make you have low self-esteem? Why didn't you make a different decision?

At the end of the day, no matter what you think about the past, what you want to change about the past, or questioning yourself on why you made a certain decision in the past, none of those thoughts are going to change anything. No matter how much you think about it, regret it, or resent it, nothing is going to change what has happened. There is no going back, no time machine, no do-overs—what happened is done, and you NEED to move on.

It may require you to forgive certain people, let go of certain grudges, or even forgive yourself for your decisions and what you allowed people to do to you. The longer you hold on, the more it is going to affect you.

Most of the time, people who have hurt you in the past are not sitting around thinking about how they hurt you. Most of the time, they do not care if they hurt you or even remember that they did.

What Forgiveness Is and What It Is Not

When you choose to forgive someone, you are choosing to let go of the things they have done to you. You are choosing not to think about them in a negative way and you are choosing not to get them back. Forgiveness is never for the other person's benefit, in fact, they usually do not know or care that you are holding a grudge. It is for you, because the only person that un-forgiveness is affecting is you.

That does not mean that forgiveness equals reconciliation. You can forgive someone from a distance. It does not mean that you need to go back to that person and give them a chance to hurt you again. If that happens, you have no one to blame but yourself. God graced us with common sense too.

Learn to forgive people and let go of the past. Do not go chasing your ex. Do not go sleeping with your ex. Do not go trying to make him be a father to a child he does not want to be a father to. Do not try to keep his child away from him, because you are mad he is with someone else. And do not hurt the father of your child, because you feel that he has hurt you. Let all of that go.

"For if you forgive other people when they sin against you, your heavenly Father will also forgive you. But if you do not forgive others their sins, your Father will not forgive your sins." Matthew 6:14-15

Day 4: *Let It Go*

Daily Prayer

Dear God,

I forgive those of my past. All of those who have hurt me and all of those that I have hurt. I pray that You give me peace and wisdom on how to deal with such people when they try to tempt me or bring me back down. I pray for Your grace when dealing with such people, so that I do not allow them to continue to cause me pain. I will not allow what people have said about me or what people have done to me continue to cause me to be angry with them. I forgive them and release myself of any anger and resentment I have toward them, just as I know You forgive the things of my past.

In Jesus' name I pray. Amen.

~Day 5~
Fight Your Demons

Demons are all around us, waiting to jack up our day and screw up our destiny. For the Bible states:

"For our struggle is not against flesh and blood, but against the rulers, against the authorities, against the powers of this dark world and against the spiritual forces of evil in the heavenly realms." Ephesians 6:12

In layman's terms, all this really means is that the devil and all his demons are wandering about the Earth, trying to figure out how to mess up your life and turn you against God. We all have demons, because none of us is perfect. But it is better to be able to see your demons for what they are, so you can deal with them. If you ignore your demons, they will continue to grow and make things worse for you.

Demons can be causing you to create your own demise. Causing you to sleep with man after man so that you can be validated by him. Causing you to think so little of yourself that you want to commit suicide. Demons can cause you to think that you are a mistake, your life is a mistake, your child is a mistake, you are a bad mother, or nothing at all. Demons can cause you to commit adultery and justify sleeping with another woman's husband. Demons can encourage you to actually hate your own children.

Day 5: *Fight Your Demons*

The thing about demons is that they think they are in charge. Because they sit around in your head and masquerade themselves as your own thoughts, until you cannot tell where you begin and the demons end. That is why you have to learn to recognize them and fight them. Recognize your power. You are of God, and you have authority over the demons and the devil. You do not just have to sit around, allowing them to stomp all over you and play around in your head.

"In order that Satan might not outwit us. For we are not unaware of his schemes." 2 Corinthians 2:11

The reason why the demons are pounding all over you and taking ahold of your life is because you do not see them for what they are. You may have been one way for so long that you do not even realize that this is not you.

Let me tell you a story. I used to struggle with lust a lot. My weakness was fine men. I struggled with lust for so long that I did not even realize I had a problem. I thought that was what normal people did. Thinking about fine men and having sexual thoughts about them. No problem right? WRONG!

These thoughts are not normal. The lustful thoughts were blinding me, changing me and the way I behaved toward men in real life. It all started in my head and was now manifesting through my behavior.

It was not until I went through my own purging with God and got rid of the lustful thoughts that I realized those were demons. I have now lived seven years without those lustful thoughts. And because I am free from lust, I have been able to be celibate for years and conquer my flesh. I am not longer allowing flesh to conquer me. You see how that works?

Are you prone to lying, jealousy, bitterness, hurting people with your words, un-forgiveness, getting back at people, meanness, anger, or having a smart mouth? These are all things that are NOT of God. They are demons that you need to rid yourself of.

According to Galatians 5:19-21, acts of the flesh (AKA demons) include:

- Sexual immorality, impurity, and debauchery: Having sex and sharing your body with everyone. Lusting, fornication, adultery, and things of that nature.

- Idolatry and witchcraft: This does not have to just be calling yourself a witch, but loving something more than you love God. Examples include money, your boyfriend, believing in astrology, consulting the stars and/or psychics about your future, valuing what you have (clothes, house, etc.) more than you value God.

- Hatred, discord, jealousy, fits of rage, selfish ambition, dissensions, factions, envy, drunkenness, orgies, and the like.

The Word is very clear on what is acceptable behavior and unacceptable behavior.

"I warn you, as I did before, that those who live like this will not inherit the kingdom of God." Galatians 5:21

Day 5: *Fight Your Demons*

Daily Prayer

Lord,

I know that I am not perfect, as none of us are. But I also know that my mission as a Christian is to try to become like Christ. Although I know I can never be perfect, I do want to rid myself of demons, attitudes, and behaviors that are of the devil. I pray that You reveal my demons to me, and I pray that You show me how to deal with my demons. I will no longer allow the devil to play games with me, play games with my life, or play games in my head; and I rebuke demons now.

In Jesus' name, Amen.

~Day 6~
No One Has Authority Over You, Declares the Lord

Forget what the world says you are, but remember who God says you are. The world can think, because you are a single mother, that you sleep around, you are struggling, you are bound to be single for the rest of your life, or you are a bad mother. Do not listen to the world. They have nothing to say about your destiny. The only one who knows about your future is God.

For He says:

"'For I know the plans I have for you,' declares the Lord, 'plans to prosper you and not to harm you, plans to give you hope and a future.'" Jeremiah 29:11

Please note that the Scripture says, *"I know the plans I have for you, DECLARES THE LORD."* Not 'declares your enemies,' 'declares the people who do not like you,' or 'declares the people who are bringing you down.' DECLARES THE LORD.

One thing I learned long ago, when enemies tried to come against me, is that they can only do what God allows them to do to me. Even when Jesus was being put on trial and the determination was being made to crucify Him:

Day 6: *No One Has Authority Over You, Declares the Lord*

"Pilate said to Him, 'Do you refuse to speak to me? Do you not know that I have authority to release you and authority to crucify you?'" John 19:10

"Jesus answered, 'You would have no power over me if it were not given to you from above.'" John 19:11

In the end, no one has authority over you. If someone is doing something to you, know that it is because God is allowing it. Even with Pilate, though he thought he had authority over Jesus, the real plan was for Jesus to be crucified so that He could serve as a savior for you and me. In the end, Pilate had control over nothing and God had control over everything.

So the next time you get overwhelmed, upset, or distraught about what people have said about you or you want to believe that you are what people say you are, remember what God says about you. God does not make mistakes. You are here for a reason, He has plans for you, and He loves you. Nothing that people say about you, what you have done in the past, or how people judge you is going to change that.

"If God is for us, who can ever be against us? Since He did not spare even His own Son but gave Him up for us all, won't He also give us everything else? Who dares accuse us whom God has chosen for His own?" Romans 8:31–33

So who can tell you anything about yourself that God does not already know? And who can dare touch and blame what God has chosen for His own? Although people may try, it is up to you to believe it or not. That is why you must look to God for your own identity and not look to other people.

God is the one who is unwavering, who will love you, and who always wants to protect you. Who else can boast that they can do such things? Not your boyfriend, not your parents, not your ex-husband, and not your baby daddy. Just God.

"And I am convinced that nothing can ever separate us from God's love. Neither death nor life, neither angels nor demons, neither our fears for today nor our worries about tomorrow—not even the powers of hell can separate us from God's love. No power in the sky above or in the earth below—indeed, nothing in all creation will ever be able to separate us from the love of God that is revealed in Christ Jesus our Lord." Romans 8:38-39

Enough said.

Daily Prayer

Dear Lord,

I know that You love me and I know that I live in a world that is not perfect. I pray that I find my identity in You and that I do not worry about what other people have to say about me or what other people have done to me. I know that no one has power over me other than the power that You have given them. Therefore, I pray that I do not worry about what other people are doing and I choose to keep my eyes on You and focused on what You are doing in my life. Not on other people. No matter what the situation I am in, You are in control. Challenges make me stronger and bring me closer to you.

In Jesus' name I pray. Amen.

~Day 7~
Don't Disqualify Yourself

As long as you are living, breathing, and waking up each morning, God is not done with you yet. A problem with most people is that they disqualify themselves when God has already qualified them. God may be tugging on your heart to start a business, move here, or do that; but so many people are afraid to move forward or step out on faith.

- *I am too old*
- *I am too damaged*
- *I don't know how*
- *I don't have time*
- *I have been married three times*
- *I could not possibly do (fill in the blank)*

All of these are excuses we tell ourselves as to why we CAN'T. And when you think of one of these excuses, you disqualify yourself, saying that God could not possibly use you, your story is over, and you might as well just sit here and settle into your mediocrity until God calls you home.

Stop selling yourself short. God decides when your story is over, not you. And as long as you live to see another day, there is still hope, there is still time to go after the impossible, and there are still dreams to be pursued and relationships to be won.

No matter who you are, what your situation is, or what you have been through, never place limits on God by telling Him that you have reached your maximum potential or you do not think you are good enough to (fill in the blank).

If God is calling you to do something, then He is fully prepared to help it come to pass. All He requires you to do is meet Him halfway. The wonderful thing about God is that He does give an A for effort. Do not think that God is just going to complete your story by you sitting there, doing nothing, complaining about how life sucks and everything has gone wrong. All you have to do is get up, show a glimmer of hope, and believe that mountains can be moved for you—and God WILL move them for you.

"For truly I tell you, if you have faith the size of a mustard seed, you can say to this mountain, 'Move from here to there,' and it will move. Nothing will be impossible for you." Matthew 17:20

Have faith. You see miracles every day. You see people live their dreams or reach their goals. So why can't it happen for you? If you change your thinking, it can be you. You have the biggest advocate on your side. God.

If there's doubt in your heart or you place limits on God, then you are stopping your own miracles. Stopping yourself from being healed or stopping yourself from moving forward. God is all-powerful and all-knowing, but do not make Him work against your own doubts and insecurities. Allow Him to do His thing in you, complete your story, and have faith that He can make it come to pass.

Day 7: *Don't Disqualify Yourself*

Case in point:

"When Jesus entered the synagogue leader's house and saw the noisy crowd and people playing pipes, he said, 'Go away. The girl is not dead but asleep.' But they laughed at him. After the crowd had been put outside, he went in and took the girl by the hand, and she got up. News of this spread through all that region." Matthew 9:23-26

When Jesus began to heal the girl, all the people who were in the room laughed at him. It was not until he sent the crowd out that the girl rose and was healed. Jesus did have the power to heal, but the crowd's disbelief kept a miracle from being performed. Don't be the reason that God cannot do the impossible in your life.

Daily Prayer

Dear Lord,

I know that You are the great I AM, You are all powerful, all knowing, and everything I need. I know that as long as I am still living and breathing, You are not done with me yet. I ask You to reveal Your purpose to me and give me the strength, knowledge, faith, and wisdom to carry it out. I trust that wherever I fall short, You will carry me the rest of the way.

I accept that You have big plans for me no matter what I have done and no matter what I have been through. I know that Your plans for me surpass any plans I have for myself. Help me believe and help me know that You can—and will—do the impossible in my life.

In Jesus' name I pray, Amen.

~Day 8~

You are Complete on Your Own

As a single mother, I think the most natural thing that so many women want to do is to hurry back into a relationship or hurry up and get a man. They miss being married, coming home to someone, or having that father figure for their children. So they rush into their next relationship or going out every night to find a man, thinking that is the key to being happy.

This behavior is a sign of the emptiness that you have in yourself and in your heart. And the only thing it is going to make you do is jump in a relationship with someone else who is probably not right for you, causing you even more emptiness.

In order to be happy as a single, you have to realize that you are enough. You should already feel happy on your own and just realize that the person you end up with will add on to your own happiness, not define it. I always tell the story that when I was single, before I had my son, I would go out a lot. I was never home, because I never wanted to be alone.

Being alone made me think about where my life was, what I was doing with my life, how alone I was, and where my future was headed. Those were all things that I did not want to think about, because if I did, I would get depressed. Because I was headed nowhere. The truth of the matter was that I was not really doing anything significant and living under what I was capable of. I felt I needed men to complete me and that is what I chased. The man, not the purpose.

After I had my son, I did not have the freedom to go out as much, and it was then that I was faced with the person I was. I realized my potential and realized that I needed to aspire higher than what I was doing. Not only for myself, but for my son. I did not have those outside distractions of going out to drown out my own voice and the voice of God.

That is when my life really started to take shape. I spent a lot of time with God. I found my purpose in God, and I found out that God had bigger plans for me than I had for myself. I realized that I did not NEED a man to complete me, that I was enough. And what God had instilled in me was bigger than what I could find in any man.

With my new-found me, I started to act differently and behave differently. How you present yourself to the world is the way in which other people perceive you. If you come across like a desperate or self-conscious woman, that is what other people will think about you. If you come across like a confident woman and a child of God, that is how people will treat you.

Let me tell you the story of the prodigal son.

"There was a man who had two sons. So he divided his property between them. The younger son set off for a distant country and there squandered his wealth in wild living. After he had spent everything, there was a severe famine, and he began to be in need. He longed to fill his stomach

with the pods that the pigs were eating, but no one gave him anything." Luke 15: 11-16

"When he came to his senses, he said, 'How many of my father's hired servants have food to spare, and here I am starving to death!'" Luke 15:17

In the story, the son finally came to his senses. He remembered who he was. He remembered that he did not have to starve, eating and picking up behind pigs. He remembered his position, and he remembered that he could go back home to a place in which he did not have to suffer like he was. He remembered that he did not have to depend on other people for food or allow other people to treat him badly. And so he decided to go back to his RICH father, and his father welcomed him with open arms.

In case you are not getting it, the prodigal son is you. Many women go out into the world searching for love in all the wrong places, looking for things to make them feel fulfilled, and allowing men to treat them badly and walk all over them. Really, all you had to do is come home to the Father to feel fulfilled. You do not need anyone else to do that for you.

So how many of us daughters of the King have gone and wasted all of our wealth and are out here living like peasants, forgetting that we are princesses? Forgetting that we have a wealthy father at home who can save us AND welcome us with open arms no matter what we have done?

It is time that you start behaving like a daughter of the MOST high God. Never think that a man or any other person should define you. You are complete on your own and the daughter of a king. Never forget that.

Daily Prayer

Dear Heavenly Father,

I know that I was fearfully and wonderful made, and if You took so much time to make me, I know that I am enough. I no longer want to live in the world and be validated by men. My only validation comes from You. Give me the confidence, strength, and self-esteem I need to realize that I am complete in You. And when I do enter a relationship, allow me to know my worth. Do not allow me to enter into bad or abusive situations, where men want to put me down and make me think less of myself. Always allow me to remember who I am and what I am worth.

In Jesus' name I pray. Amen.

~Day 9~
Enjoy Yourself

As a single mother, do you want to wait until you have the "complete" family unit before you start enjoying our life? Do you want to wait to buy a house, to travel, to purchase a new car, or to do things in your life that you feel would be better enjoyed if you had the traditional family?

If you choose to live your life that way, you will be sitting around watching life pass you by. Even if you want to be in a relationship or get married, you do not need to put your entire life on hold until that happens. The best thing that you can do is to start enjoying you, because you are a very awesome person and your life can be equally as awesome if you stop waiting and start doing.

"An unmarried woman or virgin is concerned about the Lord's affairs: Her aim is to be devoted to the Lord in both body and spirit." 1 Corinthians 7:34

If you are a single mother and have never been married or if you are divorced, then understand that marriage is not something that you just NEED to rush into. Even when it comes to divorced women, they forget how hard marriage can be, and for single women, they often idolize marriage and therefore have an unrealistic view of marriage. Thinking that when they get married, all of

Day 9: *Enjoy Yourself*

their problems will go away. And that is simply not true. Marriage brings its own set of problems.

While you are single, enjoy yourself, find your purpose, and do something that YOU want to do. Do not sit around on the couch waiting for your prince charming to come knock on your door and rescue you from your single relationship status. Life too short and too precious for that. No matter what our life situation is, tomorrow is not promised to anyone. So why not enjoy today?

"Do not boast about tomorrow, for you do not know what a day may bring." Proverbs 27:1

You do not know what the next hour, minute, or second may bring, and therefore, you should go after everything you ever wanted with all your heart no matter if you have a man or not. The last thing you want to do is to look back on your life with a whole bunch of 'what ifs' and regrets because you were just sitting around, waiting, and watching the paint on the door dry until the man of your dreams walked through it.

If you cannot learn to enjoy yourself and love yourself, then how can other people learn to enjoy you? If you want to travel more, go ahead and do it. If want to buy a house, then do it. If you want to make more money, then do it. What is stopping you?

"And don't be wishing you were someplace else or with someone else. Where you are right now is God's place for you. Live and obey and love and believe right there. God, not your marital status, defines your life." 1 Corinthians 7:17

There is much to be enjoyed during this season. Do not let your current season pass you by because you are too busy wishing for the next. Each season brings its own blessings.

Daily Prayer

Dear Lord,

I pray that I learn to be content in my position, knowing that this does not mean I will be in the same place and in the same situation forever. But right now, while I am in this season in my life, I pray that You show me what You want me to do, what You want me to learn, and who You want me to help. I do not desire to be anywhere else but in this moment with You, learning what You want me to learn and doing what You want me to do. Speak to me now and let me know exactly how I can maximize this present season in my life.

In Jesus' name I pray. Amen.

~Day 10~
Take a Look in the Mirror

Mothers tend to be so busy worrying about other people that we forget to worry about ourselves and let our appearances go. A lot of Christian women think it is very vain and superficial to take care of yourself. I am a Christian woman who disagrees with that statement. It is one thing to be vain and care so much about your appearance that you are validated by your looks, and it is another to realize that your body is a temple and it is your responsibility to take care of it.

When it comes to outward beauty, there are two verses that I want you to consider.

"Don't you know that you yourselves are God's temple and that God's Spirit dwells in your midst? If anyone destroys God's temple, God will destroy that person; for God's temple is sacred, and you together are that temple." 1 Corinthians 3:16-17

If your body is the temple of God and the Holy Spirit dwells there, then why do you want to walk around looking all raggedy and poorly kept? Some of you get dressed up for a date, so why not give the same consideration to God?

If He is in you and always with you, then take care of your appearance for Him. How can you, as HIS (meaning God) child, walk around looking a mess, knowing that

HIS spirit is dwelling in you? Having the spirit dwell in you is a privilege, so take care of your temple and make yourself look like it is a privilege for the Holy Spirit to dwell in you.

"Therefore, I urge you, brothers and sisters, in view of God's mercy, to offer your bodies as a living sacrifice, holy and pleasing to God—this is your true and proper worship." Romans 12:1-2

In Biblical times, when someone sacrificed an animal, it could NOT be some low-budget looking animal that had matted fur and was about to die anyway. The animal to be sacrificed had to be the best of the best. It had to have a pleasing appearance and be without blemish (Numbers 6:14).

So since you are offering up yourself to God, you need to look the same way. Do not offer some strung-out version of yourself before God. Do not go out in the world, telling people how full you are in Christ but looking like you held on to the bumper of a car and allowed it to drag you for a mile or two.

No one is going to believe how full you are in Christ if you look as if you are suffering. Be a living sacrifice to God. When people look at you, they should see that you look so happy, healthy, and well taken care of that they want some of what you got.

Never for one second should you think that I am encouraging you to go around and spend all of your money trying to keep up with a certain appearance. I am just saying do not forget about taking care of yourself, where God's Spirit dwells in you.

Day 10: *Take a Look in the Mirror*

Taking Care of You Means the Inside Too

Before I reached the age of 30, I used to eat whatever I wanted and could still maintain my ideal weight. But as I got older, I had to eat better, exercise more, and really take care of my temple. Because you only get one, and the last thing that you want to do is wear out your body, organs, and heart. You need these organs to live a long life. So the last thing you want to do is to wear your body out so much that it is about to give out because you are not taking care of it. You need your body to keep on working and ticking for as long as possible.

"So whether you eat or drink or whatever you do, do it all for the glory of God." 1 Corinthians 10:31

Remember your body is a temple with the spirit of God living in it. Do you want to poison it by putting a lot of drugs, alcohol, and bad food into your system?

You can take care of your kids, but do not forget to take care of mom. When you look in the mirror, you should be HAPPY about what you see.

Daily Prayer

Dear Lord,

Thank You for creating me just the way I am. I accept that my body is a temple where Your Holy Spirit resides. I pray for myself, my mind, my body, and my spirit so that it may last as long as possible. I also pray that I make the best decisions regarding my health, exercise, and diet as possible. I know that my body is a representation of You and You would want me to go out in the world with my best face forward and with a positive attitude. I pray that I not only care for my family, but for myself too. On both the inside and outside.

In Jesus' name I pray. Amen.

~Day 11~
Use What You Got

Depending on how you became a single mother, you may feel like you are always behind. I have seen some single mothers feel behind because they are not established in their careers, they want to go back to school, or they want to upgrade themselves but they do not have the means to do so.

At the end of the day, no matter what your situation is, the best thing you can do is to just use what you have and use what is around you to get what you want. I remember when I wanted to go back to school and get a master's degree and a PhD, I did not feel as if I had the means to do so. I was a single mom, I did not have the time (or so I thought). I just did not know how it would work out.

I prayed and asked God to make a way. And He did. I ended up going to an online school that was accredited. I had a computer, I had the internet, and I used what I had to get what I wanted. I did not sit around and be sad that I could not go to a university in person. I also did not complain and not do anything because I thought that it was impossible. I used what I had and allowed God to guide the rest.

Let Me Tell You What "Using What You Got," Got Me

I cannot tell you how many times I was down on my money and there were things that I needed. If I could not go to the grocery store, I would go to the Dollar Tree and get food. If I could not pay to get my hair done, then I learned to do my own hair.

I had to use what was within my reach in order to achieve my goal. Which was to eat. But see, when you use what you got, God will always meet you halfway. Instead of complaining about what I did not have, I chose to be strong and use what I did have to the best of my advantage.

During that time in my life when I was struggling but still doing what I could do, that is when God birthed a purpose in me and that is when I discovered that I wanted to help other women and other single mothers get through their hard times. A purpose that would have never been discovered, had I not gone through hard times myself. That is why you are reading this book.

And because I chose to push through instead of sitting around and complaining, God gave me a new and different direction, once I passed His test. Because I am convinced that God was waiting to see if I would use what I had, instead of complaining about what I did not have.

So do not be mad about what you don't have and just focus on what you do have. Focus on what you can do and know that it will work out for the best. Do not complain about what you don't have and how nothing is going right for you; complaining will get you nowhere. Doing is what will actually get you somewhere.

Day 11: *Use What You Got*

When you use what you have, knowing that you do not have much, you are able to make something with it. That is when you truly see the glory of God. You can see Him work with something little and make something great. But you have to give Him a little something to work with. You dig!?

Daily Prayer

Dear Lord,

I know that complaining and negative thinking are getting me nowhere. No matter what my situation is, I know that You are just waiting for me to use what I got so that I can get to where I need to be. I pray that I am able to push the negative out of mind, see my situation through Your eyes, and start doing instead of being a sitting duck. I pray that You reveal to me how I can use what is around me to reach my end goal. I refuse to be limited in thinking and in my success by believing that I do not having the means to do something. I know that You can take whatever effort I put forth and turn it into something bigger.

In Jesus' name I pray. Amen.

~Day 12~
Thou Shalt Have Boundaries

I remember when I first became a single mom, I felt like my life was over. Not in the sense that I did not enjoy being a mom, but that being a mom became my whole identity. I started to feel that I could not do this because I was a mom, I could not go there because I was a mom, and I could not have fun because I was a mom. Or so I thought.

What I learned was that, even as a mom, you have your own life and that life did not end when you become a mother. Your responsibilities have shifted, so do not misunderstand what I am saying. I am not giving you an excuse to go and abandon your children, so that you can go to whatever it is you want.

What I am telling you is that you have to remember you and you have to remember the things that make you happy. So many single mothers feel that they have to over-compensate, because they are a single mom. They feel they have to buy, spend, get the latest gadget, work 80 hours a week, and then feel guilty because they work too much and cannot spend enough time with their kids. Or they feel guilty when they cannot get their child what they want, because they do not have enough money.

In the end, if your child is alive, clothed, fed, and loved, I feel like you are doing a pretty good job. Do not get so consumed in being a parent that a parent becomes your only identity. Remember what you need is that peace time for yourself and you need that peace time to connect to God.

"But when you pray, go into your inner room, shut your door, and pray to your Father, who is unseen. And your Father, who sees what is done in secret, will reward you." Matthew 6:6

How many of you know that it is much easier to shut the door and go into your prayer room without a bunch of kids coming in after you and telling you that they want something every five minutes? I am a single mom. I am also a mom who is not afraid to take time for myself, to vacation for myself, to recharge for myself, and to take time to connect with God without interruption.

Wanting some time to ourselves does not make us bad moms, it does not mean that we do not love our children, and it does not mean that we will not win "mom of the year." It makes us honest and it makes us human.

Some mothers are so busy being mothers that they do not understand how burned out they really are. Your life did not become your child's life when they were born. It is still your life. And when they get old, they will have their own life to live. So do not be afraid to remember you and your own identity. You are someone's mother, yes, but I know you have more depth than that. Have firm boundaries with your children and do not get so enmeshed in their life that you forget to live your own life.

Daily Prayer

Dear Lord,

I thank You for my child(ren). I thank You for blessing me and giving me the opportunity to be a mother. But I also know that my whole life should not be engulfed in them. When You breathed life into me, You gave me life, and I pray for You to reveal to me how I can better use my time and do things for You and for myself. Give me an opportunity to go into my prayer closet and be able to listen and to hear Your voice loud and clear. And do not allow me to get overwhelmed in my motherly duties, but allow me to be able to have firm boundaries so I can be able to tell the difference between the lives of my children and my own life. I know that does not make me a bad mother, nor does it make me selfish, and it is okay to be a human being and to want time for myself.

In Jesus' name I pray. Amen.

~Day 13~
It is Never Too Late and You are Never Too Old

How many mothers out there feel like they have waited too long, had children too young, are too old to get married, or just too late to do what they really want to do?

As I have said in a previous chapter, as long as we are still breathing and God is waking us up in the morning, there is still time.

Case in point: I want you to read the story of Abraham, specifically focusing on Genesis, chapters 15 and 18.

One of the promises that God gave Abraham was that he and his wife Sarah were going to conceive a child. NOT only did God tell Abraham that he was going to have a child, but God made a very BOLD promise.

"And He took him outside and said, 'Now look toward the heavens, and count the stars, if you are able to count them.' And He said to him, 'So shall your descendants be.'" Genesis 15:5

That is a big promise for God to make someone who does not have any children. One may think that they would need to start having kids at five years old in order for their decedents to be as much as the stars.

As time went on and no child came, Abraham grew to be discouraged.

"Then Abraham fell on his face and laughed, and said in his heart, 'Will a child be born to a man one hundred years old? And will Sarah, who is ninety years old, bear a child?'" Genesis 17:17

Both Abraham and Sarah were senior citizens at this point. Sarah was beyond childbearing years, and I am sure they both thought they were too old to become parents. I mean, Abraham laughed when God told them that they would still have a child.

But guess what? God is not a liar, and God does not look at your age when He really wants you to do something. If He can put a baby is Sarah's womb after childbearing years, then I am sure that he can work for you too.

You can still get married, you can still have more children, you can still start a business, you can still change your career, and you can still do whatever it is that you want to do. I do not care if you are 30, 40, 50, 60 or 70. God is not sitting around, thinking about how old you are and that you are too old to do anything.

What many people do not get is, if there is a desire in your heart to achieve something, God put that desire in your heart. He is not going to dangle something in front of you and then tell you that you are way too old to have what He ordained for you.

"Because God does not show partiality." Romans 2:11

God is not sitting around, looking at you and saying that you are too old or that it is too late. God is looking at you saying, "I want (fill in your name) to do this task

Day 13: *It is Never Too Late and You are Never Too Old*

and so it is done." God is not partial and He is not going to say that this person is more deserving of a blessing because they are younger and they have more time left, or that you are not deserving of a blessing because you are too old. That's not how it works.

So do not think that, because you are aging, you are stuck where you are. Do not think that, because you did not make the best decisions in the past, it is too late for you to start over. And, most importantly, do not allow your age to place limitations on what you can and cannot do.

Daily Prayer

Dear Lord,

I know that I am still on this Earth and my work is not done yet. I pray that You give me the courage to not be afraid to follow my own path, and I pray that You give me the wisdom and the guidance that I need to do so. No matter how late I think I am in getting started, I know that Your timing is always perfect. So no matter how late I think I am, I know that in Your eyes I am exactly where You want me to be.

In Jesus' name, Amen.

~Day 14~
He Who Calls Me By Name

You would not believe how many women I have met who are just sitting around, looking lost in the sauce. They do not know what God wants them to do, and they are not trying to figure it out. They are scared to make a decision, because it may be the wrong decision. They are just stuck in the same place, not moving forward and not knowing what to do.

The wonderful thing about God is that, through Jesus, He gifted us with the Holy Spirit to come live in us, teach us, and guide us.

The way that you learn to hear the Holy Spirit is to get closer with God, and once you are in tune with God, you will be in tune with what He wants from you. Listening to God and doing things God's way is a sure way for you NOT to fail. But where people get caught up is that they do not want to listen to God, they want it their way, they do not want to be patient, and they want to do what they want to do. They ignore what God is telling them to do and then, when they fall on their face, they want to blame God.

Doing and being what God wants you to do and be is not always easy. If that were the case, then everyone would be out here doing it.

Day 14: *He Who Calls Me By Name*

"For many are called, but few are chosen." Matthew 22:14

Meaning that God is calling out to so many people, calling them by name, and they are not answering the call. Following the path of God is hard, and more often than not, God is going to put you through some pruning and grooming so that He can form a better bond with you. And not all of it is pretty, but when He is done, you will be closer to God and exactly where He wants you to be.

"'For I know the plans I have for you,' declares the Lord, 'plans to prosper you and not to harm you, plans to give you hope and a future.'" Jeremiah 29:11

Being a single mom, it can be hard because you can feel alone, like you are doing things all by yourself. It can be tempting to forget about God or be mad at God, because things are not going your way.

But God is calling out to you, and He is calling you by name. He wants to speak to you, and He wants to direct you. He may not tell you all the pieces to the puzzle, but that is where the trust comes in. You choose to listen to the Holy Spirit, knowing that God has plans to prosper you and not let you down. Even though you may not know what is on the other side of all of it, you choose to trust God's Holy Spirit anyway. And that is the basic definition of faith.

I am sure that God wants the best for each and every one of you. Single mother or not. It is important to not be weary through the process and to keep listening and keep your eyes on God. If you are willing to yield to Him, then He will take you to better and higher heights than you even thought you could go.

Single Mom Devotional

"Yet those who wait for the LORD will gain new strength; They will mount up with wings like eagles, They will run and not get tired, They will walk and not become weary." Isaiah 40:31

Daily Prayer

Lord,

You said You have plans to prosper me. I know that You call out to many people, and they do not listen. I want to be a part of the chosen. I want to answer Your call. I want the plans that You have for me, and I do not want to walk around in life not knowing where to go or what to do. I pray that You open up my ears and speak to my heart so that I can hear You and what You want me to do. I pray that from this day forward, You guide and direct my steps toward the life that You want me to have.

In Jesus' name I pray. Amen.

~Day 15~
Be the Mom They Can Look Up To

The Bible speaks very clearly on the type of woman that we should be. I encourage you to take a moment to read **Proverbs 31:10-31**, commonly titled "a wife of noble character."

I know what you may be thinking: you are not a wife YET or you are not a wife anymore. But, regardless of the "wife" title, the Proverbs 31 woman is a woman that one should aspire to be. Because she represents the type of woman that her children and her husband (or future husband) can look to up.

I want you to read the entire passage as listed above, but I will be taking bits and pieces of it for you to pay attention to.

Do not be lazy

"She gets up while it is still night; she provides food for her family and portions for her female servants." Proverbs 31:15

This is not to say that you have to stay up until 2 am and then rise at 4 am, just that you need to be a responsible mother. As a single mom, we have all had days where we just wanted to sit around and do nothing. Sometimes you can have those days, but do not neglect your responsibilities and do not neglect your role as a mother.

"She sets about her work vigorously; her arms are strong for her tasks." Proverbs 31:17

As a single mother, I have worked more than my fair share, I have earned my master's degree and my PhD, and I held a job while doing it. Am I saying that you need to be like me? No, I am not. What I am saying is that you should work hard. You should want your children to see you work hard. Not only will it make them want to work hard too, but hard work will always lead you to success.

"She watches over the affairs of her household and does not eat the bread of idleness." Proverbs 31:27

What goes on in your house should be your own business. Never let your children run around your home and tear your stuff up, while you sit there and do nothing. And if they are old enough, they need to have chores to help you around the house.

You should not be the single mom who is allowing boys to spend the night in your daughter's room. You should not be the single mom who does not know what is going on in your own house. You should not be the single mom who lets your children run the house instead of you.

Invest

"She considers a field and buys it; out of her earnings she plants a vineyard." Proverbs 31:16

"She sees that her trading is profitable and her lamp does not go out at night." Proverbs 31:18

I am not telling you that you need to go out there and buy a whole bunch of stocks and bonds. What these versuses speak to is that you must learn how to use your money wisely and not spend it on things that will turn you no profit.

I will use myself as an example. I am a blogger. I take personal pride in my blog, and I work very hard on it. When I am not working on my blog, I spend time and sometimes money, energy, and effort learning more about blogging, so that I can improve the way I do things. What I am trying to say is that these are all profitable investments that will service me well in the future. Now, turn that situation back on yourself.

- Do you spend money on things that will not earn you a return?
- Do you spend all of your money instead of saving?
- Do you need the latest fashions, shoes, and that is where all of your money goes?

None of those things will make you better. You cannot live in them. You cannot drive to work with these things. And you cannot send your children to college with them. So is it really a profitable investment? Whenever you make household decisions, determine if the decision is helping your household or hurting it.

Do not be selfish

"She opens her arms to the poor and extends her hands to the needy." Proverbs 31:20

One thing that really gets under my skin is when Christians do not want to help anyone. I am not saying that you have to empty your bank account and give all your money to the poor. But people should be able to tell that you are Christian, without you saying it.

They should be able to tell based on how kind you are, how you treat people, and how you act. Always choose to be kind, professional, and handle yourself with class.

Be prepared

"When it snows, she has no fear for her household; for all of them are clothed in scarlet." Proverbs 31:21

Winter comes every year and, therefore, it would not be wise to have your heat turned off right before a big snowstorm. Or get into a car accident right after you let your car insurance lapse. Granted, we cannot be prepared for everything, but we should still try our best to prepare for the things we can.

Be the woman who everyone wants to be

"A wife of noble character who can find? She is worth far more than rubies." Proverbs 31:10

A ruby is actually more rare than a diamond. Imagine how much we value diamonds, and a woman of good character is worth more and is rarer than that. That is how you should act, and that is how you should come across to other people. Like a gem, not a cheap knock-off that is just trying to imitate a gem.

"She is clothed with strength and dignity; she can laugh at the days to come." Proverbs 31:25

You should have confidence when you speak and when you walk. As a single mother, you have hidden strength. Even though you may get down and out, do not stay down and out. Be strong, have dignity, and laugh at whatever comes your way. Because as long as God is for you, then who can be against you? Knowing this alone should help you live with no fear.

Day 15: *Be the Mom They Can Look Up To*

> *"She speaks with wisdom, and faithful instruction is on her tongue." Proverbs 31:26*

One thing that you have to master in your tongue. People often think that going off on other people is a strength, but what that shows is lack of self-control. It is better to speak wisely and professionally to people. Even when people try to upset you, you should know how to articulate your words in a manner that demands respect and is not demeaning.

> *"Charm is deceptive, and beauty is fleeting; but a woman who fears the Lord is to be praised." Proverbs 31:30*

I personally believe in being beautiful from the inside out. But in the end, you are not going to be young forever. Your beauty will fade as you get older, but one thing that should never fade is your belief in God and what He can do for you. Even though we waiver, God doesn't.

Daily Prayer

Dear Lord,

I pray to You to transform me into the woman that You want me to be and the woman that my children can be proud of. If there are things that You want me to work on, I pray that You let me know what they are and give me the necessary insight and guidance. You clearly describe the type of woman who gains favor in Your sight, the Proverbs 31 woman. I pray that I am able to transform into that woman, and more than anything, I pray that I always remain in awe and recognition of You and Your greatness.

In Jesus' name, Amen.

~Day 16~
Keep Peace in Your Home

I am going to describe a few situations that you may have encountered as a single mother, which kept you from having peace in your home.

Situation #1: You are so busy working and too exhausted to deal with your children. So they run around like wild animals and you let them.

Situation #2: You feel guilty that you are a single mother and therefore allow your children to run all over you. You feel sorry that they do not have the traditional family, and you excuse their behavior because they "have no home training."

Situation #3: You are your children's friend. You do not want them to be mad at you, you do not want to tell them no, and, more than anything, you want to be the cool mom who allows them to do whatever they want to do without limits.

Your situation can be all of these, a little bit of this, none of this, or a combination thereof. But as a parent, it is your responsibility to keep the peace in your home.

If your children are running around, wreaking havoc on anything and everything that they come in contact with, then you need to figure out how to get your situation under control. Single parent or not, you are a parent, and it is your responsibility to do what you need to do to rear your child the right way.

When you think about how the Lord deals with you, do you think that the Lord wants you running around, acting crazy, disrespecting people, and tearing stuff up? NO. So therefore, you need not let your children do it.

"Endure hardship as discipline; God is treating you as His children. For what children are not disciplined by their father? If you are not disciplined—and everyone undergoes discipline—then you are not legitimate, not true sons and daughters at all. Moreover, we have all had human fathers who disciplined us and we respected them for it. How much more should we submit to the Father of spirits and live! They disciplined us for a little while as they thought best; but God disciplines us for our good, in order that we may share in His holiness. No discipline seems pleasant at the time, but painful. Later on, however, it produces a harvest of righteousness and peace for those who have been trained by it." Hebrews 12:7-11

This message is trying to tell you that you do not need to sit and try to be your child's friend over their parent, you do not need to allow them to run all over you because you are a single mother, and even in the days that you are tired and do not feel like dealing with their nonsense, you need to put them in check. It is your job as a parent.

I am not going to tell you how to discipline your child, but just know that not teaching children to respect you, your home, or the things that you have worked hard for will come back and bite you. Not teaching your children that they need to respect authority and adult figures will come back to bite you too.

Day 16: *Keep Peace in Your Home*

Your children should fear you in the same way that you fear the Lord. Not in the sense that they are scared you are going to kill them, abuse them, or something crazy like that. But more in the sense of reverence and respect.

Daily Prayer

Dear Lord,

You gave me the blessing of having children and I pray that You give me the wisdom and the strength to teach them how to grow into children that love the Lord and have respect for me and others. I pray that I have peace in my home and I can show myself as a woman of good character, one my children respect, help, and value.

I reclaim myself as the adult in the home and know that I am worthy of being respected and revered. In whatever area I am lacking, I pray that You help me overcome it and give me strength when it comes to disciplining and rearing my children.

In Jesus' name I pray. Amen.

~Day 17~
Train Your Child

"Train up a child in the way he should go, and when he is old he will not depart from it." Proverbs 22:6

When children are born, they are always learning and absorbing. Which is why training starts from birth. You cannot be a neglectful mother and then wonder what happened when your child turns 16 and he or she does not respect you or talks to you any kind of way.

It is because you never trained them. If you ask me, I will tell anyone that it was never too early to train my son. Even as a toddler, he pushed my limits, and I let him know that the world has rules and in this house he obeys mine. When people look at my son, they think, "Oh you are lucky, because your son is so well behaved." No, I made him well behaved.

From the moment that children are born, they are selfish. They do not care if you are sleepy; they are going to cry in the middle of the night. They do not care if they should eat vegetables; they would rather eat junk. When they do not get what they want, they fall on the floor and start throwing tantrums.

But as a parent, you need to not tolerate that. In this world today, there are all these stipulations in being a parent and allowing your children to roam free, figuring

Day 17: *Train Your Child*

out the world on their own. People want you to think that it is your job as a parent to provide all these "feel good" moments.

And this is why we have a bunch of kids who cannot cope with everyday life. Allowing your children to just do what they want and how they want will not do you any favors. And it is against the Bible. Because the Bible knows that training starts very early. If you instill values and respect in your children, then that is all they will know.

I have been very blessed to be able to send my son to a Christian school since pre-k. When my son once asked to go to public school, I ask if he knew that children could not pray in public school. He was shocked and distraught! How can anyone NOT allow prayer to God?

The concept was so abnormal to him that he did not even understand it. I often envy my child's relationship with God at such an early age. Because he started talking to God early, he prays about everything. My son will think about praying for something even before I will. That is what training your child early will get you.

It is not like one day he just woke up and started a relationship with God. I helped him, his school helped him, and the people that he encounters help him form that relationship. Early on, he formulated a relationship with God, was taught the importance of God, and seeks to go to God for everything. Because that is what he has been taught.

The same can be said for teaching your child to work hard. If you never make your child work, aspire to reach a goal, or try harder when the going gets rough, then that will be their life. Whenever school or jobs are hard, they will quit because you did not train them.

Everyone wants their child to grow up and be the best adult they can be. That is why the training has to happen early. And do not let anyone tell you that, because you are a single mom, you are not equipped to teach your child alone. Do not let anyone tell you that, as a single mom of a boy, you cannot raise a man. I simply do not believe that. There may be some single mom reading this book, knowing that her child's father is not a man. Knowing that he cannot do better in raising her child if he tried. That is where you come in.

They have a Godly father and with God as your helper, you can raise a boy to be a God-fearing man AND you can raise a girl to be a God-fearing woman. Train them up. Start very early, and they will not depart from it.

Daily Prayer

Dear Lord,

I thank You for giving me my child(ren), and I want my child(ren) to grow up and become God fearing. I want to train them up in the way that they should go, and I look to You in order to find out how to do that. I pray that You are always with my child and convict them when they are thinking of wrongdoing. I pray for myself as a parent and that You give me guidance on how to bring my child up so that, when they are older, they will never depart from You.

In Jesus' name I pray. Amen.

~Day 18~
Stop Caring About What Other People Think

There are so many people in the world who care too much about what people think. I personally never understood it. In the end of this journey that we call life, other people are not the ones who are going to be looking at you on judgment day and holding you accountable for your sins. God is. So who cares about what other people think?

Who cares about what they think about you, what they think about your situation, what they think about you being a single mom, what they think about how you became a single mom, and any other tidbits that they think about you that are not productive to your life? Who cares? Do not love the world or the things in the world.

"If anyone loves the world, the love of the Father is not in him. For all that is in the world—the desires of the flesh and the desires of the eyes and pride in possessions—is not from the Father but is from the world. And the world is passing away along with its desires, but whoever does the will of God abides forever." 1 John 2:15-17

This verse is not to say that you should just go around hating everything in the world, including the people it in. But rather how you should feel about what the world has to offer. For the most part, people of the world do not stand for the same things that God stands for.

People of the world stand for being naked all over social media, fighting on television, telling people off, and being sexually promiscuous. That is what the world stands for, which is why you cannot worry what the world thinks about you. Because the world is not going to get you into Heaven, only Jesus can do that.

"Do not be conformed to this world, but be transformed by the renewal of your mind, that by testing you may discern what is the will of God, what is good and acceptable and perfect." Romans 12:2

The closer that you get to God, the more you realize what God wants for you versus what other people want for you. If I were to listen to what other people wanted for me, then I would not be where I am today. People told me that I could not go back to school as a single mom, let alone earn a PhD. Yet, here I am. That is because I did not listen to people, and I did not listen to the statistics about single moms getting advanced degrees. What I did listen to is God, and I allowed Him to guide my footsteps and give me the future that He has in His mind. I did not listen to anyone else.

I know that there are so many people around you that may be talking about you, talking behind your back, keeping you down, or telling you that you can't. But in the end, those people have no authority over you. Remember:

"You would have no power over me if it were not given to you from above." John 19:11

Know that no one has authority over you and the only power that anyone has is the one given to them by God. And even in those instances, they do not have free will to do just anything to you. They can only do what you let

Day 18: *Stop Caring About What Other People Think*

them do and what God allows them to do. So do not let them get in your head and affect you or your direction.

Daily Prayer

Dear Lord,

I know that I have validation in You and You are the only validation that I need. I know that I do not need to pay attention to anyone else in this world, especially if they are trying to bring me down and not lift me up. What I do pray is that You bring positive people in my life that are of You. Those that are going to encourage me and not discourage me. And if there is anyone in my life who is bringing me down through their action and words, keeping me away from Your purpose, then I pray that You remove them from my life, so that I can focus more on You and what You have for me. If there are people who I know are a bad influence and I am afraid to not have them in my life, I pray that You give me the wisdom on how to deal with them and cut them out of my life if need be.

In Jesus' name I pray. Amen.

~Day 19~
Fear Not, for Fear is Not Perfected in Love

As a single mother, I have gone through so many things, especially when it came to money. I never really got a steady stream of child support, mainly because my child's father was in prison for seven years after my son was born. After I got laid off from my job, the only emotion I felt was FEAR and ANXEITY.

I felt fear when I heard a truck in my neighborhood, thinking they were coming to turn the lights off because I was late paying my utilities. I felt fear over not knowing how I was going to get food or pay my son's tuition so that he could keep going to school. I was a nervous wreck about any and everything. Because everything was going so wrong, and I did not know what tomorrow would bring, I felt fear and anxiety. All of the time.

Even though that was a hard time in my life, I literally lacked for nothing. We always had something to eat, and I had the basic utilities that I needed. I feared, because I did not know. I did not know how, when, or what, so that made me afraid.

But despite the fact that was a terrible time in my life I would NEVER want to repeat, it was the time in my life where I learned not to fear.

Day 19: *Fear Not, for Fear is Not Perfected in Love*

The Bible teaches us:

"There is no fear in love. But perfect love drives out fear, because fear has to do with punishment. The one who fears is not made perfect in love." 1 John 4:18

This was a hard lesson to learn. Even when I had no job, when it took me so long to get another one, and when I was underpaid and still struggling. It took years to get to a spot where I did not feel like I was broke all of the time. But in the midst of that emotion, I stopped fearing.

I learned that no matter how many things were not going the way I wanted them to, worrying did not change anything, nor did it get me anywhere.

"Can any one of you by worrying add a single hour to your life?" Matthew 6:27

What does worrying get you? It almost got me a nervous breakdown, and I am not being funny. I was a nervous wreck. But what can you change by worrying? If they were going to turn my lights off, then they were going to turn my lights off. Me worrying was not going to fix that. What was going to fix it was trusting in God. Because God was the one that provided for me the entire time, despite my worrying and nervousness.

"Therefore I tell you, do not worry about your life, what you will eat or drink; or about your body, what you will wear. Is not life more than food, and the body more than clothes? Look at the birds of the air; they do not sow or reap or store away in barns, and yet your heavenly Father feeds them. Are you not much more valuable than they?" Matthew 6:25

Even though, as a single mom, life may be uncomfortable and scary, God tells us not to worry. He tells us to be like the birds that just know they are going to get a next meal. So if we are more important than a bird, then we should not fear about what God is doing and how God is doing it.

If you are in a position like I was and all you do is worry about what the future holds, don't. Fear is not perfected in love, and if there is something you need then just ask God. I have seen and experienced miracles. Ways to pay bills that I did not think I would be able to get paid, people gifting me with things that I prayed for, reminders that even though I was not in a comfortable spot, God had not forgotten about me.

And in the midst of this hard time was a lesson. To not fear man, to not fear the world, and to not fear what the world is doing. God has the ability to protect you from all that nonsense and lift you out of whatever gutter you are in. It taught me, that when I am experiencing something hard, to go to God first and to not have fear about the trouble in my life or what the future holds.

Daily Prayer

Dear Lord,

You know the situations I am facing in my life. You know my fears, my anxieties, and my concerns. I know that by worrying, I am not doing myself any favors, and this is the perfect opportunity to take the burden off myself and to put all of my cares and concerns on You. Help give me the comfort in understanding that You can fix whatever burden I place before You. I release my worry and my concerns to You.

In Jesus' name I pray. Amen.

~Day 20~
Wear Your Crown

Do you remember the story of Tamar? If you are not familiar with the account of Tamar, daughter of David, let me give you a brief overview. David had a few wives, and Tamar was one of David's daughters. Amnon was Tamar's half-brother from another wife. Amnon grew an infatuation with Tamar, which turned into lust.

Amnon wanted to have sex with his half-sister, but he knew that he could not just up and do it, so he had to trick her. One day, during dinner, Amnon told David that he was too sick to come down and the only thing that could make him feel better was for his sister, Tamar, to come up and feed him. David sent Tamar to Amnon's room and then Amnon raped her.

"Then suddenly Amnon's love turned to hate, and he hated her even more than he had loved her. 'Get out of here!' he snarled at her. 'No, no!' Tamar cried. 'Sending me away now is worse than what you've already done to me.' But Amnon wouldn't listen to her. He shouted for his servant and demanded, 'Throw this woman out, and lock the door behind her!' So the servant put her out and locked the door behind her." 3 Samuel 13:16-18

After the rape, Tamar begged for her brother to marry her. Even though she had been raped due to no fault of her own, she was now considered spoiled and could not get married, since she was no longer a virgin.

In this instance, you see that Tamar felt she was no longer a princess and so she ripped her royal robes. We also know that Tamar went on to live as a desolate woman. But let me ask you this: just because Tamar ripped off her own royal robe, did that make her any less of a princess? No, she was not a virgin, but was she still not royalty? The last thing I want you to consider is why she allowed her half-brother to take away her entire life and make her go on as a desolate women, never to be seen or heard from again. The rape was wrong, but happened after the rape and the fact that Tamar decided to just disappear did not have to happen.

Tamar was still a princess, no matter what happened to her. And the fact of the matter is that no one else ripped off her royal robe but her. She thought that her half-brother robbed her of her royal position and she had no choice but to go hide herself away like she no longer mattered.

I know often times as single mothers we can feel like, because we have a family or a child already, it takes away from what we can do, what we can aspire for, how people see us, or even our prospects for a relationship. We sit and blame ourselves for situations that we put ourselves in and things that we have been through. Like Tamar, we consider ourselves as less than worthy.

She let what happened to her get her so down and out that we never hear from her again. Could she not believe that no one wanted to be with her despite her being raped? She allowed her sick, rapist brother to take away

Day 20: *Wear Your Crown*

her royal position. Tamar was still a princess, she still had a crown, and she was still the daughter of David, but she chose to give up her crown because of what someone else did to her.

Don't be Tamar. We have a past, none of us are perfect, we have made some mistakes, and sometimes we have even wanted to crawl away into obscurity. But do not let anyone banish you off your thrown.

You are the daughter of the highest King, and you need to act like it. No matter what your past is, God is not sitting around thinking of what or who you used to be. He is sitting and thinking about where you are going. But if you rip off your royal robes and just go hide away like Tamar, then you will never know what the future holds for you.

There is nothing to be ashamed about. As long as you have confessed your sin, God will forget all that you have done as far as the east is from the west (Psalm 103:12). So do not count yourself guilty for things you have already confessed, do not see yourself as anything less than the child of God, and more than anything you need to FIX your royal crown. Put it back on your head and reclaim your position on the throne.

Daily Prayer

Lord,

I come to You today as a humble child of God. I know that I am Your daughter, and I pray that You give me the wisdom of who I am and who I am destined to become. I go forward from today with a new identity in Christ, which is a princess. I accept my royal position and will begin to act like I am Your child. No longer hiding in shame and no longer allowing other people to tell me that I am not royalty. I take Your hand and I step on the throne today. The throne that You built for me when You sent Your son Jesus to die for my sins. I accept my royal position.

In Jesus' name I pray. Amen.

~Day 21~
Decorate Your Temple

God warns us from becoming too obsessed with our looks, because looks are fading and they will not be with us forever. I do agree; I think that becoming OBSESSED with your looks and thinking that your looks are all you have to offer people is not what God wants. But as a Christian woman, I personally do not think that there is anything wrong with caring about your outside appearance.

"Do you not know that your bodies are temples of the Holy Spirit, who is in you, whom you have received from God? You are not your own." 1 Corinthians 6:19

When I used to live in Europe, I saw many religious temples and cathedrals that were hundreds of years old. And they were all kept in amazing shape. I could tell they VALUED that temple based on how they kept it.

Imagine if I would have walked in a temple and it was cracking, falling apart, and stones and rocks were coming down on my head as I walked through the temple. I would have wanted to run out of there for fear that something may collapse on my head. I would wonder why on Earth they kept this place of worship in such terrible condition.

What I am trying to say is that there is a difference between a well-kept, beautiful temple and one that is falling to the ground. The one that is beautiful says "I am valued, I am treasured, I want to look good for a long time, and I am aware of how I come across to the world."

If God thought so much as to sculpt every aspect of you, then why would you not think so much of yourself to take care of each aspect of you? Often times, as single mothers, we neglect our outward appearance and our temple, thinking that because we do not have time, it is okay to step out of the house looking any kind of way. It is not okay. What if you met someone that day who could give you a better job and you were looking crazy? Or if you met someone who was your future husband and you were looking crazy?

Why would you want to take that chance? That is not to say that we get dressed for other people, because we don't. We get dressed for ourselves, because like those churches in Europe, we should take care of God's temple.

Daily Prayer

Dear Lord,

I know that You formed me from my mother's womb, and You put every part of me together. Including my hair, my nose, my feet, my face, and my body. I want to choose to honor You in all ways, including my appearance. When I get dressed and leave the house in the morning, I want the world to look at me and see a child of God, who cares about her temple and who is a representation of how the Lord wants me to look.

In Jesus' name I pray. Amen.

~Day 22~
Be Healthy

Remember the last chapter, when I was saying that your body was your temple and you should take care of the outside of it? There is no point of having a pretty outside if the inside is all rotten and filled with mold.

Imagine you are hungry, walking in a desert, and you come by a piece of fruit that looks so beautiful on the outside. You pick up the fruit to take a bite, only to find out that it is molded in the middle. How much of a disappointment would that be? Don't be that fruit. Don't be that woman who puts a lot of effort into her outward beauty, but on the inside you are falling apart.

I used to be this person. Eating whatever I wanted and, because I still looked great on the outside, it did not really bother me much. But then I hit 30, it became harder and harder to stay in shape and that is when it hit me. If I wanted my body to last for years and years to come, I needed to watch what I put into it.

Read the story of Daniel:

"Daniel made up his mind not to let himself become ritually unclean by eating the food and drinking the wine of the royal court." Daniel 1:8

You see, the king had ordered all the men to eat and drink things that were probably not very healthy, and Daniel did not want to do this.

Daniel said:

"'Test us for ten days,' he said. 'Give us vegetables to eat and water to drink. Then compare us with the young men who are eating the food of the royal court, and base your decision on how we look.' He agreed to let them try it for ten days. When the time was up, they looked healthier and stronger than all those who had been eating the royal food." Daniel 1:12-15

Am I telling you that you need to become vegan? NO, I am not. But we cannot deny what Daniel was saying, that eating vegetables and drinking water is important to our health. If God thought so much to put it in the Bible, then it must be important to him too.

True story: Once, as I was praying to God about not eating a cookie, I asked God why He had to make all the good things bad for you. As soon as I ask it, God revealed something to me.

God told me that the things that he created were the things that we see growing out of the ground. The fruits, the vegetables, and the animals. Nowhere in the Bible does it say that God created processed sugar and all this stuff that we eat and is bad for us.

Those are all man-made things. Am I saying that you can never have sugar? NO, I am not. But to eat bad foods to excess, consume sugar to excess, and drink alcohol to excess will just wear your body down. And it is not what God wants for us or our bodies.

Day 22: *Be Healthy*

Take a note from Daniel and start eating more naturally produced things. Like fruits and vegetables and water. Be kind to yourself and take care of your insides. You only have one body, and the last thing you want to do is to wear it down before its time. The more you take care of it, the better it will be to you.

Daily Prayer

Dear Lord,

I know that in the world in which we live there are too many temptations for food. I know that having bad eating habits and eating the wrong things is not only detrimental to my body, but it is also not what You intended. So I pray that You break the strong holds that I have to food, alcohol, or even tobacco and teach me how to be kinder to my body. I know that Your Holy Spirit resides in me, and I would not want to make my body a toxic place but rather a healthy and enjoyable place for it to love. Help guide me to a healthier lifestyle.

In Jesus' name I pray. Amen.

~Day 23~
You Can Still Have Your King

You may be a widow, a divorced mom, or a single mom who has never been married. No matter what your situation is, you can still have your king. God never said that because you are a widow, because you have never been married before, or because you are divorced you can never be married to a good man ever again.

To prove my point, I want us to take the case of Ruth. I encourage you to read the entire Book of Ruth if you are not familiar with it.

Ruth was a Moabite and a widow. So was her mother-in-law, Naomi. Here were these two widows, Ruth never having a child and Naomi having two boys (both dead), both feeling like their lives were over.

To make a long story short, Ruth did find her Boaz. In her older age, she found a man that was good for her and she had children. Did the fact that Ruth found Boaz mean that she did not love her deceased husband? No, it did not. Did the fact that Ruth was once a married woman diminish her worth in the eyes of Boaz? No, it did not. Never think that your situation as a single mom is not fixable and that you cannot have a happy ending. You can.

Day 23: *You Can Still Have Your King*

At the conclusion of the Book of Ruth:

"The women said to Naomi: 'Praise be to the Lord, who this day has not left you without a guardian-redeemer. May he become famous throughout Israel! He will renew your life and sustain you in your old age. For your daughter-in-law, who loves you and who is better to you than seven sons, has given him birth.' Then Naomi took the child in her arms and cared for him. The women living there said, 'Naomi has a son!'" Ruth 4:14-16

Not only was Ruth happy, but also Naomi, in her old age, found herself to be fulfilled. She too was a widow who thought she would never have a family or a child, and she was redeemed with her daughter-in-law and her grandson. So single moms, you can have a king, you can have a family, and you can have a life. Do not think that, because you are single mom, you are not worthy or that you already had your chance.

Daily Prayer

Dear Lord,

I know that You do not judge me for me being a single mom and that I am deserving of a king just as much as any other woman. I will not think that being a single mom means that I cannot get married or that I cannot find happiness with a man. I know that I can, and I know that I can do it with You by my side. Help me see myself as worthy of getting a king and help me be patient until a king finds me.

In Jesus' name I pray. Amen.

~Day 24~
Guard Your Heart

"Above all else, guard your heart, for everything you do flows from it." Proverbs 4:23

When you read the Bible, there is so much that God has to say about guarding your heart. The above verse is just one of those things. When you are a single mom, you need to watch what and who you let into your heart.

This can be true when you start dating again. The last thing you want to bring into your heart and your home is a man who is no good, leaving a lasting impression on your heart and the heart of your kids.

"A good man brings good things out of the good stored up in his heart, and an evil man brings evil things out of the evil stored up in his heart. For the mouth speaks what the heart is full of." Luke 6:45

So allowing a lot of sex and lust into your heart will not work. And allowing a lot of people to deposit a lot of bad things in your heart will not work, because what is in your heart will come out of you in one way or the other. And if what is going in is bad, then what is going to come out will be bad too.

Just a few weeks ago, I was in a situation with a bunch of new acquaintances going to happy hour. They were acting how I used to act, very toxic and very foul mouth,

Day 24: *Guard Your Heart*

AND I allowed them to take me there. Because I was hanging out with these people, after about an hour or so, they deposited little things in my heart that made me act like them. Like someone I thought I had changed from. Like someone I did not want to be.

And this is why we have to watch the company we keep. This is why we cannot be in relationships or friendships with people who encourage us to do the wrong thing. Have you ever heard the old saying "birds of a feather flock together?"

That is because people you hang out with rub off on you, leaving deposits in your heart. If they are good, it is easier for you to be good. If they are bad, it is easier for you to be bad. Guard your heart.

Daily Prayer

Dear God,

I want to begin to guard my heart. I pray that You show me who in my life is good for me and who is bad for me. I pray that You allow me to see people's true intentions and whether they are making me a better person or a worse person. I also pray that I am able to recognize if I am putting bad deposits on other people's heart and assist me in changing the type of person I am so that my behavior can reflect what my heart is full of. I give You permission to transform my heart.

In Jesus' name I pray. Amen.

~Day 25~
With God's Help

As a single mom, there are all types of stereotypes about what you cannot do or how you are not going to make it. And often times, as single mothers, we believe that we are limited because of our single-mom status. I remember when I used to have such small-minded dreams. Then one day, during my prayer session, God told me that I needed to dream bigger.

I went back and forth with God for a while, until I realized that I was limiting my own self. I was limiting myself for being a single mom, I was limiting myself because of what I thought I could and could not achieve, and I was limiting myself based on the things that I thought were and were not possible. But there is one thing that I did not account for and that was God.

"And those whom He predestined He also called, and those whom He called He also justified, and those whom He justified He also glorified. What then shall we say to these things? If God is for us, who can be against us? He who did not spare His own Son but gave Him up for us all, how will He not also with Him graciously give us all things? Who shall bring any charge against God's elect? It is God who justifies." Romans 8:30-33

God has called you out. He has called you by name, and if He sees you as fit to live the life of your dreams, then

Day 25: *With God's Help*

no one is fit to tell Him differently. If He sees fit to give you the man of your dreams, then who is anyone to tell Him differently? If He sees fit to give you the house of your dreams, then who is anyone to tell God differently?

God already believes that you are capable of the impossible, but do you believe? Do you know that you can put a damper on God's plans due to your wavering faith? God cannot take you to new places and new heights if you do not think that you belong there.

> *"For all the promises of God are 'Yes' in Christ. And so through Him, our 'Amen' is spoken to the glory of God." 2 Corinthians 1:20*

All this means is that God is saying yes to you. Yes to your heart, yes to getting married, yes to finding a good man, yes to finding a better life, and yes to that new job. But in order for it to come true, you have to add your AMEN.

There is nothing like watching God take someone from glory to glory. Someone that you never thought would be taken from glory to glory. It is in those instances that you can really see how God can work in someone's life. Because he chose to take someone that the world sees as being on the bottom and put them on top. And that person can be you.

Daily Prayer

Dear Lord,

I know that You have a wonderful life for me. It does not matter what I have done in my past or that I am a single mother; there is nothing about me that limits my success. I choose to believe You, the life You have for me, and that You can go above and beyond all the things I have ever prayed for and imagined. I pray that You allow me to dream again, and I know that if You are giving me a dream, then Your answer is already yes. I am adding my amen.

In Jesus' name I pray. Amen.

~Day 26~
Satan, Get Behind Me

You know the best revenge on anyone who said you would not amount to anything? Just be better than before.

I cannot tell you how many people have tried to hold me down or hold me back. The end results are that I am where I am and they are still sitting where they were, hating on my success. That is because I realized a long time ago that it is the devil in people that makes them want to hate you and makes them want to hold you back.

Before you go around, calling people the devil, you have to realize that sometimes people do not even realize that they are the devil or doing the devil's work.

Case in point:

"From that time on Jesus began to explain to his disciples that he must go to Jerusalem and suffer many things at the hands of the elders, the chief priests and the teachers of the law, and that he must be killed and on the third day be raised to life. Peter took him aside and began to rebuke him. 'Never, Lord!' he said. 'This shall never happen to you!' Jesus turned and said to Peter, 'Get behind me, Satan! You are a stumbling block to me; you do not have in mind the concerns of God, but merely human concerns.'" Matthew 16:19-23

Can you imagine the look on Peter's face when Jesus called him Satan? But see, Satan was working through Peter, and he did not even know it. We all know that Jesus had to die, and that was the only way for you and me to be forgiven of our sins. But had Peter convinced Jesus out of his death, then Christianity would have been null and void.

That is why it is so important not to listen to other people about their plans for you and your life, or to allow them to make you feel bad for what you want to do. Do not sit and spend time engaging in their foolishness. Do not even argue with them. Tell them, "Satan, get behind me," and keep going higher, rising higher, and doing better.

The more you focus on other people and what they think about you, the less time you have to really focus on yourself and do the things that are best for you and your kids. The biggest thing that you can do to prove people wrong about you and shut them up is to keep doing you and keep doing better. Stop caring about what other people have to say about you and tell them to get behind you. The only place that you should see people who are not for you is in your rearview mirror.

Daily Prayer

Dear Lord,

I pray that You are able to let me recognize who is for me and who is against me. I also pray that I am able to ignore those who are against me, despite what they say about me. I am telling Satan to get behind me. He has no authority over me, he has no authority over my life, and

Day 26: *Satan, Get Behind Me*

he has no authority over my children. I rebuke anyone or anything that is trying to keep me from becoming my absolute best or from making my life better.

In Jesus' name I pray. Amen.

~Day 27~
Be Better Than Before

I have always told people that I am not the same person I was 10 years ago. BUT it was not like one day I just woke up and I was some transformed person. Instead, the transformation took place a little at a time. When you submit to God, He is going to want to change you for the better, not all at one, but little by little.

God transforms us using small and gradual steps, because if we were to look at the end goal, we might get discouraged that it is too great or too far away. That is why taking small steps is better. To start that process, all you have to do is wakeup and tell yourself that you are going to be better than yesterday, that you are not going to make the same mistakes, or that you will be a better mother than the day before.

Often times, as Christians, we can use the grace of God to stay in our nonsense. We will tell ourselves that, since Jesus died for our sins, we can just ask Jesus for forgiveness when we sin. As a result, we use this grace as an excuse to do the same thing, time and time again, committing the same mistakes and never getting better.

The first thing you have to understand is that you need to stop using the grace of God as an excuse to sin. Yes, Jesus does forgive us, but do not insult Him by openly sinning in His face and then pleading the blood of Jesus,

Day 27: *Be Better Than Before*

knowing full well that you are going to commit the same sin again tomorrow.

Yes, humans make mistakes and sometimes we make mistakes over and over again until we get it right. But we should at least try to get it right. At least try to be better than before. Try to make one less mistake. Try to a little harder not to sin. Try to little harder not to make excuses for your behavior. Try a little harder not to get caught doing the same dumb thing that landed you in the same bad position in the first place.

And it is those very small steps that make you better than before. The more you reject the wrong way of doing things and embrace the right, God will start to convict you. He will start to make you better and you will start to see the error of your ways.

I used to be a partygoer. I used to do A LOT of things wrong. And I remember knowing that they were wrong and also NOT wanting to give up that lifestyle. It was way too much fun.

But my desire to please God overrode my desire to do what I wanted to do, because doing what I wanted to do was getting me into a lot of trouble. So as I submitted to God, He started to change my heart and He started to change the way I saw things.

No longer did I feel that my ratchet behavior was the fun thing to do. I started to see the stuff I was doing through God's eyes, and as a result, I stopped doing them because I saw how reckless it was to my own wellbeing.

No, it did not happen all at once. But all I had to do was try to be better than before. One minute at a time, one hour at a time, and one year at a time. I just had to focus on being better. Until, 10 years down the road, I am nowhere near the person I used to be. AND I have a better life than I thought I could ever have.

Listen to God and start to make small changes in your life. Even though you may not want to give certain things up, do it anyway. Not only is it good for you, but God will reward you.

Daily Prayer

Dear Lord,

I pray that my heart becomes Your heart and my desires Your desires. Through this process, I know that You will allow me to become a better woman than before. I am a woman after Your own heart, and I want to do right by You. I know that I will not wake up and be transformed by tomorrow, but give me the grace to do it one day at a time. To change one day at a time. If there are any ways in my life that You want me to give up, then I pray that not only will You reveal them to me but You will give me the grace to do it.

In Jesus' name I pray. Amen

~Day 28~
Relationship Advice from Queen Esther

One of my favorite books of the Bible is Esther. She is literally an orphan who becomes a queen. So if you are a single mom and you think that you being a single mom is going to keep you from a good man, then you are wrong.

When you read the Book of Esther, you can clearly see that God had a plan for her. God can work His magic in any way possible to ensure that you end up with the man that He wants you to end up with, as well as the life He wants you to end up with. Esther went from being an orphan to being a queen.

Consider these things when it comes to Esther:

"Now the king was attracted to Esther more than to any of the other women, and she won his favor and approval more than any of the other virgins. So he set a royal crown on her head." Esther 2:17

I know often times, as a single mom, you may want to get married and you may even wonder if it is going to happen. Do not get into the habit of chasing men or doing something desperate for the attention of a man. If you desire to get married, there is a man out there for you. You will not have to worry about a man not wanting you, not being seen, or being judged by your past. You will not have to worry about trying to do tricks or playing games to catch the man you want, he will just want you for you.

Remember, in the Book of Esther, when she was afraid to tell the king that she was Jewish? And when she finally did, that it really did not make one bit of a difference? It did not make the king love her less and it did not make him want to banish her as queen.

A real man who loves you and is destined to be with you is not going to judge you because you are a single mom. If anything, he will embrace you AND your children, because your children came from you.

It is sad to say that so many single mothers, in the effort to get married or to end their relationship status, jump into wrong relationships.

But because they want to feel loved or wanted, they take attention from anyone. As a single mom, I need you to believe that God can pluck you from anywhere and even out of obscurity and that he will give you a king to be a good man and father figure to both you and your children.

I also need you to believe that the time will come when the time is right and if you try to force that, then you will only be causing pain for yourself.

Case in point:

"Before a young woman's turn came to go in to King Xerxes, she had to complete twelve months of beauty treatments prescribed for the women, six months with oil of myrrh and six with perfumes and cosmetics." Esther 2:12

Before Esther became queen, she did not just walk in there and automatically become queen. It took a lot of

Day 28: *Relationship Advice from Queen Esther*

training and it took a lot of preparation. She knew that she had to wait 12 months before going before the king.

So there was no use after month one going before the king, knowing that she was not ready and knowing that she did not finish the right preparation for the king. So, instead of focusing on the relationship and focusing on the king, focus on the preparation. Do what you need to do to be fit for a king.

Second case in point:

"And Esther won the favor of everyone who saw her." Esther 2:15

I remember, when I was reading the Book of Esther several years ago, this was the Bible verse that stood out to me the most. And what I thought about the most was that Esther's reputation must have preceded her.

I can only imagine that, before the king met Esther, he heard other people singing her praises. Because Esther was a good person and she had a great personality (or so I speculate). But whatever it was about her, people liked her and they enjoyed being around her.

And this may have been one of the reasons why the king chose her. If you want to get married or be in a relationship, do not be some nasty, cold-hearted woman to everyone. You do not know who is looking at you and you do not know whose favor you may catch.

Your reputation should be good and your reputation should precede you. It would be hard for any man to approach you or even your friends to want to introduce you to someone if you are known for being nasty.

Take a lesson from Esther. Be a woman who is kind, who has a good reputation, and who has gone through the preparation to meet her king. And trust that, in the right way and the right time, God will bring you a king.

You do not need to go down the path of chasing men and being desperate to find someone to love you. That will happen automatically with the right man who wants to love you the way that God loves you.

Daily Prayer

Dear Lord,

I know that You have created the sacrament of marriage and You know that it is my desire to one day be married. I trust You with all areas of my life, including my relationship status. And I know for a fact that You have a wonderful man in store for me. What I pray now is that You reveal to me the areas that I need to improve on and the areas in my life I need to prepare. And, while I am getting in the right place for a relationship, I pray that You give me the peace to be patient in waiting for the right man. And I pray that You will bring a good man into both my and my child's life.

In Jesus' name I pray. Amen.

~Day 29~
Lessons from Ruth - God is in Control of Your Love Life

What we can learn from Ruth is that God is still in control of your love life. It does not matter if you have been divorced or even if you have been widowed; there is still life for you left to live.

Ruth was married before, and her husband died. She followed her mother-in-law to a city that she did not know and did not even know what awaited her there. For all she knew, she was a stranger and no one would want anything to do with her.

Historians agree that Ruth was about 40 years of age when she met Boaz. Forty is not old, but in that day and age, 40 was old enough to not have any children and to be embarking on your single life again. So I am sure Ruth may have set out to this new city to just live out the rest of her days and die.

She probably had no hope to have children or to get married again. But, low and behold, God had another plan for her. Ruth was just minding her own business, working hard in the field, and that is where Boaz noticed her.

That is when her whole life changed and she went from a mourning widow to a woman of wealth and a mother.

So what am I trying to say? Your life is not over until God says it is over. As long as you are still here and breathing, there is still hope for you yet. Never think that, as a widow or even a divorcee, you can never be in another relationship and you are never going to be happy again. Never think, because bad things have happened in your life, your life is over and nothing can ever get better.

That is not true, you can choose to believe this and also give yourself permission to not feel guilty for it. And lastly, never think that, because you are a single mom with children, no man is going to ever want you and your relationship status is hopeless.

The fact of the matter is that there are single mothers who have been widowed, divorced, and single for a very long time, and they have found their Boaz. What we can learn from Ruth is that God cares about your relationship status, he wants you to be happy, and no matter what happened in your past relationships you can have a good future relationship. I encourage you to read the Book of Ruth on your own and see how God worked in her life.

Daily Prayer

Dear Lord,

I come to You today as a new woman, knowing that no matter what pain, suffering, or breakups I have gone through in the past, they do not determine my future. Just like Boaz found Ruth, I trust that the right man will find me at the right time, and I believe nothing that has happened in my past can keep me from having a wonderful future. I pray that You guide my love life just like You guided the life of Ruth. And no matter how old I am, it is never too late.

In Jesus' name I pray. Amen.

~Day 30~
The New You

Today is the last day of this devotional. Through these chapters, I wanted you to really have a reflection. I wanted you to be a new person AND a better person than when you first began this book.

Often times, single moms feels like they are struggling, like things are not going to be better, and like they do not have any friends or time to date. But in the end, I hope that these devotions not only gave you encouragement BUT also gave you hope. Hope for your future and hope that God is on your side. He is your Father and, no matter what your situation, God has no limitations. He does not see you as beneath anyone or as less than worthy of anything.

The new you means that you need to start seeing yourself from God's eyes and finding your identity through Christ. Not through the world and not through your situation, but through God's eyes.

The wonderful thing about God is he loves to use very imperfect people to do his purpose. So, as you go forward during the day and in your life, know that God is on your side.

I cannot overemphasis that point. You do not need people, a man, friends, or an ex-husband to really do anything for you, because you have the most powerful Father EVER! These people can be in your life, but you do not need to lean on them for everything regarding your life. That is what God is for.

As you walk through life, walk with God, see yourself through His eyes AND find your purpose in Him. Remember, with God, you are a new being. I pray that this devotional has given you the courage and encouragement to go to God with everything. I also pray that through these devotions, you have received new revelation and renewed faith on what you are capable of and the type of life God wants you to have.

Daily Prayer

Dear Lord,

I want to go forward as a new being and a new person with the identity that You have given me. I pray that I always walk with You, and I pray that I will always talk to You as I know You call me by name and I am Yours. I know that You have a wonderful life planned for me and will give me the desires of my heart. I trust You completely, I trust what You have planned for me, and I pray that You do work in me so that I can be in a position to receive the life You have for me.

In Jesus' name I pray. Amen.

Closing Thoughts

I really do hope that you got encouragement from this devotional as a single mom. But just because the book is over, who says the party has to be? In case you could not tell, I really love encouraging women, and I am so honored that God called me into this purpose to encourage each and every one of you.

With that being said, I write regularly on my blog, so please pay it a visit. Even though this book is over, you can head over to www.sophie-sticatedmom.com and become a regular part of my crew. On my blog, you can became a part of the Sophie-stication Nation (which is my awesome email list) and get more personal tidbits, newsletters, and other free stuff that I do not post on the blog.

Don't forget to stay in touch. Feel free to follow me on Instagram, Facebook, Twitter, or YouTube. Whatever your social media fancy, I have it, because I love keeping in touch and connecting with you.

Until we meet again, stay blessed.

Made in the USA
Columbia, SC
11 May 2025